MW01233611

Dre Baldwin

This Month's Contents

Support: Team@WorkOnMyGame.com | WorkOnYourGameUniversity.com | Text:1.305.384.6894

WORK ON YOUR GAME
UNIVERSITY

This Month's Theme: Difficult But Critical

Almost everyone I talk to is seeking higher levels of "productivity."

People want to get more done, in less time, so that theoretically, we can move ourselves forward, faster – before our time runs out.

This is a good idea.

One problem: Human nature.

Human nature moves us to lean towards doing things that are easier to do, and to

do more of those things, so we are "productive" – the question is, productive _at what_?

The paradox of this whole thing is, we can do _fewer_ things – being LESS "productive" – however, choosing the few things that are both critical and important to our forward movement and success.

In other words, doing things that are _effective_, not just productive.

Productive: _having the quality or power of producing especially in abundance_

Effective: _producing a decided, decisive, or desired effect_

It's good to be productive. It is better to be effective.

When we are chasing productivity, we are looking to get as much done as we possibly can. But the fact of the matter is, the most important things to get done usually number in the few, and if we get those essential few things done, we move ourselves forward much more quickly than when focused on the trivial many.

In this way, less effort produces more outcomes.

Support: Team@WorkOnMyGame.com | WorkOnYourGameUniversity.com | Text:1.305.384.6894

WORK ON YOUR GAME
UNIVERSITY

So, then, why don't we do this more often? Why doesn't everyone do this?

Good question. Here's the answer.

It's that the important things that we need to do – the essential few – are usually not easy to do.

They require a lot of thinking.

They require a significant amount of effort.

They often push us out of our normal modes of operations and comfort zones.

They don't fit in with our current set of habits.

That's exactly why we need to do them.

The difficulty of doing the essential few is not that we don't have the capability, it's just that they require adaptation of a different state of mind, and the divorcing from our normal modus operandi.

The critical part is, these are the things that take us where we want to go, and do so much faster than doing a plethora of the trivial stuff that we habitually busy ourselves with on a daily basis.

So, here's where you start with this: Get conscious about the unconscious.

Notice yourself defaulting to your normal habits of doing "productive" things that don't really produce a result.
Instead, now that you're thinking about it, challenge yourself to focus on doing the few things that make a big difference, but you are not predisposed to want to do.

This is where big changes and big jumps happen.

Yes, this has been available to you the whole time.

But, you know what they say about the best time to plant a tree…

— Dre Baldwin

Support: Team@WorkOnMyGame.com | WorkOnYourGameUniversity.com | Text:1.305.384.6894

WORK ON YOUR GAME
UNIVERSITY

6 Business Things Every Author / Coach / Speaker MUST Know

A "Thought Leader" is a person who trades in intellectual property; i.e., you take your knowledge, experience, perspective and insights and sell them in the form of books, coaching, consulting, training, courses, etc.

When people buy from you, they're not buying a physical item (though you may have tem) as much as they're buying the transformation that comes from what you'll share.

For example, I sell books - but you're not paying $20 for the pages and ink. You're paying for the result of what will change in your life from reading the book. The physical book itself (or audiobook or digital book) are merely the medium for getting the message to you.

What you're reading is directed specifically at those working in this space.

These are the six KEY things you must not only know, but understand and apply to your business.

1) The most important thing you do is give value while selling NOTHING.

I spent my first 5 years online in this mode.

I was sharing basketball training tips and drills with up and coming players who were ambitiously looking to move forward in the sport. I didn't have anything to sell, and didn't even know how to sell anything online, even if I had had something to offer.

You don't need to take that long. You can give value mixed in with selling. The only reason I went as long as I did without offering anything to sell is because I didn't know what I didn't

know. But, that "unconscious incompetence" served me, because when I finally did have something to sell, I had a hungry and ready audience that already knew me, liked me, and trusted me – which made my sales immediately take off.

What made my sales take off was not the amazingness of my product, but the 5-year investment I had made into my audience while asking for nothing in exchange.

I built such a strong base with my audience that many would stay with me for years, even as I pivoted to more of a mindset focus, then into entrepreneurship, and then dropping basketball as a topic altogether. Many of those original audience members are still reading my articles to this day.

By the way, this was all via word of mouth. I launched my first-ever ad campaign in 2018 or 19. Before that, my audience grew simply because the people who found me, then told their friends about me.

Putting out good material that a specific audience badly wanted was my entire marketing strategy.

Now, let's talk about why they were telling their friends about me…

2) Building the know / like / trust connection makes selling easy.

My first products — two skill-based self-training programs for basketball players— sold immediately. I already told you why: I'd built a strong relationship with my audience over several years. I was giving them value and asking for nothing in exchange. I did so for so long, that when I did finally ask for something in exchange, it was a no-brainer for my audience.

This is not to say my audience felt like they owed me something; just to be clear. It is because I had a dialed-in offering that supplied my audience EXACTLY what they needed and solved the EXACT problem they knew they had.

How did I do that?

Because: I had spent so much time dealing with my audience that I knew exactly what they needed. I wasn't guessing as to what to sell to them; they had already told me. I read all the comments, emails and DMs. Due to this focus, coming up with an idea was EASY. Plus, my audience didn't have to question if they could trust me or if I knew what their problem was; they already knew the answers to both of those questions via the free stuff I'd been putting out.

Support: Team@WorkOnMyGame.com | WorkOnYourGameUniversity.com | Text:1.305.384.6894

WORK ON YOUR GAME
UNIVERSITY

Are you seeing how these pieces fit together?

Let's keep going…

3) Even AFTER you're selling stuff and making money, you need to keep doing points 1 & 2.

Keep dealing with your audience, giving them value, responding to their challenges and questions.

Why? Because they are telling you what the NEXT thing is that they will need after the last thing you gave them.

For example, I'd given aspiring basketball players training programs to get better at dribbling, shooting, dunking, etc. Guess what they wanted next? A program for getting their bodies in shape. Then they wanted the mindset to help put all this stuff into action.

Guess what I created next? Exactly what they asked for. Do you think it sold well?

As long as you are paying attention, actively listening, and staying engaged, you will know exactly what your audience needs next.

The biggest challenge I see with this for some is that you are talking to too many different people, who have disparate needs and challenges. Therefore, you get confused as to what you should do next, because there is more than one answer.

The Solution: Get focused on who your IDEAL client is.

If you could pick just ONE of your customers, out of all of your audience, who is the ideal person? If you had a thousand customers FOR LIFE, but the catch is they are all the same as ONE person, which customer would you pick to clone 999 times?

Which product, service, or offer would you stick with, if you only had to sell only ONE?

The answer to these is where your focus should be; everything else should support and grow out of that, or go away. This level of focus is what many entrepreneurs lack, and it's the reason why many entrepreneurs can work really hard – yet never get close to achieving their goals.

Focus is a force multiplier. Distraction is a force divider.

Now, let's talk about some harsh truths about the thought leadership business…

Support: Team@WorkOnMyGame.com | WorkOnYourGameUniversity.com | Text:1.305.384.6894

WORK ON YOUR GAME
UNIVERSITY

4) You're targeting 2-5% of the population.

That's all, amongst 8 billion, that will actually want + consume + apply what you share.

(Some larger percentages may want + consume but will not apply).

Understand what you're actually doing: You are sharing knowledge, information, and material that helps people GET better and DO better. Most people are NOT interested in that!

Changing people's thinking is an exercise in futility; I'd suggest you stay out of that business and focus on the already-converted. Stupid people tend to stay stupid. Poor mindsets tend to remain that way. There are exceptions, of course – exceptions PROVE the rule, not debunk it.

You are in the business of finding those who are already aligned; i.e. who WANT to get better and are willing to invest in doing so, and preach to that choir. So you have to be smart and selective about choosing where you go, who you're talking to and who you're attracting.

(By the way, 2% of 8 billion is 160,000,000 people. There IS a market for us.)

On that note…

5) Who you are is more important than what you sell.

You are not the only person on the planet talking about the topic that you're talking about.

I didn't invent practicing basketball. I doubt anyone would say I'm the best player in the history of the game. But I built an audience and a business doing it – because the players connected to me the PERSON just as much as (if not more than) me the PLAYER.

Today, there are lots of people talking about mindset. Many more talking about business. A lot of talking about how to make more money. There are tons of relationship coaches, a whole bunch of personal trainers, nutrition experts, and thousands talking about some aspect of development and growth.

None of us is 100% unique. Which means, you will not, and should not try to, separate yourself by simply being "better" than the others. Most people cannot objectively tell who is better than the other anyway, and frankly, most people don't care.

Support: Team@WorkOnMyGame.com | WorkOnYourGameUniversity.com | Text:1.305.384.6894

Burn this on your brain: People choose you based on WHO YOU ARE, not the quality of your stuff.

The quality of your stuff is secondary. Maybe even tertiary when we consider how you present yourself. You are in the self-aggrandizement and personal marketing business as well as the thought leadership business.

Your background story (and how you tell that story), how you present yourself, and the thoughts / emotions / reasons behind what you do matter MORE than your "expertise."

I know this firsthand.

Let me tell you what people tell me when I ask them, "why me?"

"You're honest and direct."
"I like how you keep it real."
"I like how you get to the point."
"You say things that people are afraid to talk about."
"Your delivery style resonates with me."

Notice what they DIDN'T say:

"You're the best basketball player I've ever seen."
"You invented discipline, confidence and mental toughness."
"There are no other entrepreneur coaches alive, so I had no other choice."

This should create a HUGE shift in focus for many of you.

6) The most important point: You are in business.

Specifically, the marketing and sales businesses.

The only way money moves in your world is for you to market and sell something to someone.

It is only THEN that you get to do your thing – whether that thing be speaking, coaching, healing, mending relationships, helping people lose weight, etc. You can't do that thing that you love or are great at, UNTIL you sell something.

This is why, as a thought leader, you need to focus on the BUSINESS more than you need to get better at doing the thing.

Translated with an example: Your ability to sell yourself as, say, a professional speaker, is more important than how good you actually ARE on the stage as a professional speaker. Because if you can't SELL yourself into a speaking gig, it doesn't matter how good you are – because you'll never be on a stage.

Do you get it?

8

WORK ON YOUR GAME
UNIVERSITY

Most thought leaders mistakenly focus so much on their ability at the thing – but not nearly enough on the BUSINESS. This is why their business doesn't do as well as they want them to do. If you want your business to do better than it is doing right now – regardless of where it currently is – your focus needs to be on getting better at BUSINESS, not getting better at the THING that you serve with.

This is the mindset of the entrepreneur vs. the mindset of the artist.

Support: Team@WorkOnMyGame.com | WorkOnYourGameUniversity.com | Text:1.305.384.6894

WORK ON YOUR GAME
UNIVERSITY

What A "List" Is  (And Why You Need One)

Business is a "contact sport."

Meaning, in order to do business, you need to be making contact, consistently, with people who could – or may in the future – be interested in giving you money.

The best way to make contact with any person, for any reason, is to connect as directly as possible.

In person.

On the phone.
Email.
Physical mail (higher open rate than email).

The mistake people make – which doubles as YOUR opportunity – is that most people would rather make contact indirectly.

People choose this, because indirect is easier, there is less chance for rejection and discomfort, and because everyone else does it.

These are three great reasons to NEVER do something.

1) It's easy.
2) Low chance of failure.
3) Everyone else is doing it.

The opportunity is always in the opposites.

Since business is a contact support, you need to be consistently in contact with your people – people who have already purchased from you, AND people who could buy in the future.

Because if you are not in contact with them, it's easier for them to forget about you – and thus, when they are ready to make a move, you will not be the first person on their mind.

10

This is a failure on your part. A failure to maintain your relationships.

If you get my emails, you see how often my name pops up in your inbox. You don't need to publish as often as I do, but you MUST be consistent – and, more importantly, you need direct access to your audience.

Translated: You must be able to reach your audience WITHOUT going through social media.

Why?

Because Facebook, Youtube, Twitter, LinkedIn, TikTok, Instagram, and everyone else has complete control over how, how often, and how easily you can reach "your" audience.

Here's a rule of life.

If someone else controls your access to something that you call "yours," it's NOT yours. It's theirs. They are letting you borrow it.

This is how social media works.

You don't "have" followers on social media. Instagram and TikTok have followers; they let you borrow them for as long as you play by their rules.

I'll prove it to you. Delete your account on one of those apps. What happens to your followers?

Nothing happens to them. They're still there. Which means they're not yours. If they were yours, they would leave with you. Social media is borrowed land. You own NOTHING.

But, on the other hand, when you have direct access to your people – via phone number, email address, or physical address – you can reach them without social media as a tax-collecting middleman.

So, if your social media accounts get hacked, you get banned off of a platform, or social media itself gets hacked, you are not shit-out-of-luck when it comes to reaching your audience.

You may think that it's impossible for social media to go away or be somehow unaccessible. It is VERY possible for it to happen, and it has happened (to people and companies) in the past. It's happening to someone today. You want to make sure it's not you.

If every social media application got deleted today, or they all banned together and decided to kick just me off of their platforms, I still have direct access to my audience.

Support: Team@WorkOnMyGame.com | WorkOnYourGameUniversity.com | Text:1.305.384.6894

WORK ON YOUR GAME
UNIVERSITY

I can send you an email.
I can text message you.
I can send physical mail to your house.

Why? Because I have all that information from you.

That information is what we call a "List."

A list just means, people who have given you their direct contact information, and with it, the implicit permission to reach out to and market to them.

The list is the most valuable asset a business owns.

Eight years ago, Facebook tried to purchase Snapchat for $3 billion. Snapchat refused the offer. Why did Facebook offer $3 billion for an app that, as was proven shortly thereafter, they could easily copy on their own (this copy became Instagram Stories), with their own in-house team of engineers?

Good question. Here's the answer.

Because Snapchat had a list that Facebook wanted access to. Young, social-media-savvy, and heavy social-media-using youth are Snapchat's users.

Facebook was willing to pay $3 billion for it. It wasn't for Snap's technology. Facebook could develop that on their own.

A few years before that, Facebook purchased WhatsApp for somewhere between $16 and $19 billion, depending on who you ask.

Why? For the exact same reason.

This is the power of the list.

Understand that your list is more than just the names, numbers and email addresses; it is the relationship you have with the people on the other end of that information. That relationship is worth a lot of money, because when you have a relationship with an audience of people, they usually listen to what you have to say, and if your stuff is any good, they buy it.

This is how you could sell your business in the future. But, ONLY if you have the relationships.

This is especially important for those of us in the thought leadership space (authors, coaches, speakers, etc.). We don't usually have proprietary technology. Anyone can copy our information and concepts.

Support: Team@WorkOnMyGame.com | WorkOnYourGameUniversity.com | Text:1.305.384.6894

WORK ON YOUR GAME
UNIVERSITY

Which means, the day after you die, the majority of your business becomes worthless.

Unless.

Unless there's a strong relationship between you and your audience, to where someone can pick up where you left off, and the business can continue.

The fact of the matter is, this rarely happens.

I know, on very good knowledge, that many well-known thought leaders – famous people whose names you know – after they passed away, the value of their businesses went to damn near zero.

These are people whose talks, speeches, and stories still circulate on social media to this very day.

But, since they did not do the work of building a solid relationship with an audience that they had control of, and direct access to, without the main person around, there was no business.

Their concepts are great, the stories amazing, and their theories will be taught forever. But, none of that equates to business.

They had no list, and no direct relationship.

YOU need a list. You need to build a relationship with that list. Maintain your relationship with that list. Now, and forever.

If you do one thing in your business on a consistent basis, this is the thing to do.

Not writing more books.
Not creating new courses.
Not recording more videos for YouTube.
Not doing more live streams.

Building direct access to an audience of people who want to hear from you and have given you permission to continually market and sell your stuff to them.

This makes a sustainable business.

Support: Team@WorkOnMyGame.com | WorkOnYourGameUniversity.com | Text:1.305.384.6894

WORK ON YOUR GAME
UNIVERSITY

3 Days With A $10 Million Company…

I recently spent three days in Atlanta with a company that I've collaborated and partnered with on multiple projects.

First thing first: How I came to even be working with this company.

We reached out to them.

That's how it happened.

Every single day at Work On Your Game Inc., we do outreach. That means cold-contacting anywhere from 3 to 30 different entities, looking for ways to collaborate, sell our stuff, and simply make the Work On Your Game philosophy known to people who otherwise did not know about it (such as our target's audience / customers).

This is a huge part of what we do, and what I've always done in business.

Collaboration is a shortcut to success. You're using the legwork that others have already done — and they're using yours — for mutual benefit.

When I license the use of the "30 Days To Discipline" program to someone else, their clients learn the system — and I get a whole new set of eyeballs on my and my work.

Win-win-win.
Me-collaborator-client.

You'll read more about outreach as you continue this article.

With that out of the way, I want to share some insights and observations that I picked up over these three days. This is all just from watching, engaging, and asking questions.

A few things before we begin.

Support: Team@WorkOnMyGame.com | WorkOnYourGameUniversity.com | Text:1.305.384.6894

WORK ON YOUR GAME
UNIVERSITY

- This is a sales company; their focus is on helping their clients sell more and do so effectively.

- They have 21 employees, with many people wearing multiple hats.

- They're privately owned, and have been on the INC 5000 (fastest growing companies) list three years running.

1) Consistent Outreach Is REQUIRED.

The trainers and sales people at this company – as it is a sales company – are required to make 100 "outbounds" (my verbiage, not theirs) every single day.

An "outbound," for those unfamiliar, means you are doing some form of direct outreach to a person who is or may become willing to do business with you now, or in the future.

This company has four or five full-time trainers/sales people, each doing 100 outbounds per day.

What do you think their sales pipeline looks like? I promise you it's not empty.

2) Professional Studios, Cameras, Technology — And The Professionals To Operate It.

The bulk of my work over these three days was in recording, being interviewed, and taking photos. The company has an entire team of people whose job is to make sure this stuff runs smoothly, cleanly, and as it should – while staying on-time and on-schedule.

If you are in the content creation space, you understand the value of having great technology and equipment (cameras, lights, sets), and people who make that technology work the right way.

This company has a whole team of these folks, working full-time.

(They said I was the most efficient and easiest-to-work-with of anyone they've had visited before. But maybe they just said that because I was there ●)

3) The Main Guy Outworks EVERYBODY.

I spent a lot of time hanging with the company owner's Executive Assistant (EA).

An EA is a professional's right-hand person, whose job is, as I tell my own EAs, anything and everything that makes the main person's job easier.

The EA I interfaced with here knows the main guy's entire schedule, and is his

15

direct liaison for everything. If you're ever trying to reach an in-demand person, their EA is either your best shot or your worst enemy (they are experts at both opening doors and locking gates).

Being here, I asked a lot of questions about the main guy and how he does what he does.

It was told to me — emphasized, actually – that this guy is on the road 80% to 90% of the year, routinely works 16- to 17-hour days, and, from what I could observe and infer, probably puts more time into his work than all the people who work for him.

That should tell you something.

4) They Are Always Expanding.

Although I am the one who reached out to them initially to start our relationship, it was the company who reached back to me to further the relationship (which led to my trip).

I have licensed some content from my own programs and training materials for this company to use as part of their training materials. From what I saw, they are constantly looking for others like me who can add value to their existing (and future) clients and customers.

The point is, they are not just keeping all of their material to themselves. They are actively expanding and collaborating with others, finding a way to create mutual benefit for the company, their collaborating partners, and their clients.

This is how you thrive in business.

5) Be Proactive When You See Opportunity.

This point is more an observation of me than of them, and pertinent to the story.

At the end of my three days hanging with the company, I asked their EA what ways I could further engage with their company and add them even more value from my end.

This is important, because it doesn't happen if you don't ASK.

As such, I have a call scheduled for tomorrow with the main guy about exactly how we will do that.

Whenever you come across an entity — whether company or person — who is playing your game at a higher level than you, there's an opportunity in front of you. Ask a simple question: How can I further engage with you / add more value?

16

The person or company will probably have an answer, even if they don't come up with one on the spot (which means you must follow up). And, I will bet that most times, they will not come to you asking this. You must go to them first by proposing it.

Opportunity does not "knock." It wanders around, waiting for you to take initiative. Do not wait for them to come to you, you go to them.

***

Collaborating and integrating my stuff with other entrepreneurs and businesses has been one of my best advancement strategies, both in drawing attention and generating revenue.

Would this help your business?
Do you have value that you know would benefit others — but don't yet have their attention?

There is a shortcut to making this happen.

Support: Team@WorkOnMyGame.com | WorkOnYourGameUniversity.com | Text:1.305.384.6894

Referrals: Why You Should Send Your Friends To Us

Most of our best members come via referral. That is, those who already know us bring their friends!

You can help your friends discover the keys to unlocking ultimate career success and mental dominance with Work On Your Game University's Exclusive Membership.

Work On Your Game University is the ultimate resource for ambitious individuals; who in your circle has your same drive?

As you know, with our exclusive membership, they'll gain invaluable insights, strategies, and tools that will help them not only make more money, but also develop an unbeatable mindset that sets them apart from the competition.

And, there's something in it for you: A 40% commission when you refer your friends!

Yes, you get PAID to bring others in to join the ranks of Work On Your Game University members who are unlocking the secret to career success and mental domination.

You're already experiencing the incredible benefits firsthand. Now you have the opportunity to share this life-changing experience with your friends. Imagine the satisfaction of watching your friends transform their lives, all while earning additional rewards for yourself.

So, start spreading the word and reap the benefits!

With Work On Your Game University, you'll gain access to a goldmine of knowledge and resources that give anyone a serious edge in the competitive world of business and the race to success.

Our membership offers you the opportunity to:

1. Master your strategic skills and perform consistently.

18

2. Develop a winning mindset that attracts success and abundance.

3. Learn expert strategies for creating multiple income streams within your business.

4. Crush self-doubt and build unshakeable confidence.

5. Access exclusive training materials to propel your career forward.

Eliminate the Frustration and Pains of Stagnation.

Do any of your friends mention being tired of being so inconsistent? Frustrated by their lack of progress in climbing the success ladder?

With our membership, they can finally break free from the chains of mediocrity and achieve the success they've always dreamed of, just like you have. Say goodbye to stress and hello to winning!

Experience the Unlimited Payoff:

1. Earn your worth and live a life of abundance.

2. Unlock the secrets to mental dominance.

3. Gain the confidence and certainty to take calculated risks.

4. Enjoy the freedom to pursue your passions without financial constraints.

5. Create a legacy of wealth for future generations.

Share the link below with your friends to discover the unlimited opportunities that await in Work On Your Game University.

http://www.WorkOnYourGameUniversity.com/refer

Support: Team@WorkOnMyGame.com | WorkOnYourGameUniversity.com | Text:1.305.384.6894

WORK ON YOUR GAME
UNIVERSITY

5) The Bible

Books I'm Currently Reading

I tend to read 2 to 5 books at a time, between digital, physical, and audiobooks. At some point, I will re-publish my recommended reading list on my website with active links to all the books I've read, at least the ones that I can remember and track down.

Here's my current active list (and books completed in the last month), as of this printing:

1) The Robert Collier Letters - Robert Collier
2) Car Guys And Bean Counters - Bob Lutz
3) 1001 Ways To Market Your Books - John Kremer
4) My Life And My Work - Henry Ford

Support: Team@WorkOnMyGame.com | WorkOnYourGameUniversity.com | Text:1.305.384.6894

WORK ON YOUR GAME
UNIVERSITY

Get Into The Work On Your Game System

5 Steps To Increase Your Income Year-Over-Year and Be A 7-Figure Earner Without Sacrificing Your Life (Even if You Feel You're Already Maxed Out)

If you received this magazine as a gift or borrowed it from a friend, your next step is to get into the Work On Your Game System, where you'll plug into the fully codified process that I translated from the top 1% of professional sports to be used in business and life by people just like you.

Here's just SOME of what you get…

- **8 Weeks Of Coaching With Dre Baldwin** so you can get all your questions answered about how to implement the system and have strategies that apply to your specific situation…

- **Get the "Kick in the Ass" You Need to Stay On-Point** so you can stop procrastinating and stick to your commitments – which means you're actually getting things done now, instead of procrastinating and making excuses…

- **Be Supported + Held Accountable** and bring your challenges and burning questions so you're never "on an island" doing everything alone…

- **Have a Streamlined Process** which means no more randomness and hoping things work – so you'll have the clarity you need to go to work with confidence…

- **Apply a Framework That Blends Personal & Professional Development** which helps you build yourself to keep up with the growth of your business – and that means you're no longer the bottleneck holding your business back…

Support: Team@WorkOnMyGame.com | WorkOnYourGameUniversity.com | Text:1.305.384.6894

- **Access All Of Dre's Best Self-Learning Material** dig into 17+ years of training on-demand so you can work at your own pace – and enjoy lifetime access to it all…

Get started with a free training at http://WorkOnYourGame.net

Support: Team@WorkOnMyGame.com | WorkOnYourGameUniversity.com | Text:1.305.384.6894

WORK ON YOUR GAME
UNIVERSITY

[In Case You Missed It] MasterClasses

[All courses and trainings are accessible at
http://www.WorkOnYourGameUniversity.com/member

MasterClasses are on your favorite podcasting apps AND at http://WorkOnYourGamePodcast.com]

#2847: Why You Fear Success [Part 5 of 10]
#2846: Why You Fear Success [Part 4 of 10]
#2845: Why You Fear Success [Part 3 of 10]
#2844: Why You Fear Success [Part 2 of 10]

#2843: Why You Fear Success [Part 1 of 10]
#2842: Why Some People Always Win – And Others Always Lose
#2841: How To Communicate Concisely
#2840: How To Get The "Second Dollar" In Business
#2839: Why You WANT To Be Emotional
#2838: Traits Of The Top 2%
#2837: The 6 Pieces Of A Successful Book [Part 2 of 2]
#2836: The 6 Pieces Of A Successful Book [Part 1 of 2]
#2835: How To Never Get Punked Or Bullied In Life
#2834: How To Create Your "Blue Ocean" In Business
#2833: The Inequality "Gaps" That No One Talks About [Part 3 of 3]
#2832: The Inequality "Gaps" That No One Talks About [Part 2 of 3]
#2831: The Inequality "Gaps" That No One Talks About [Part 1 of 3]
#2830: Eclectic Input: Why To Get Info & Insight From Unique Sources
#2829: The Slow Bus To Success (And How To Get Off It)
#2828: What Does Seeing Other's Success Mean To You?
#2827: Everything You Believe About Marketing Is WRONG [Part 7 of 7]
#2826: Everything You Believe About Marketing Is WRONG [Part 6 of 7]
#2825: Everything You Believe About Marketing Is WRONG [Part 5 of 7]

Support: Team@WorkOnMyGame.com | WorkOnYourGameUniversity.com | Text:1.305.384.6894

Support: Team@WorkOnMyGame.com | WorkOnYourGameUniversity.com | Text:1.305.384.6894

Your Work On Your Game Journey

1) Get The Free Books

The baseline tools that are the foundation of what we teach.

http://ThirdDayBook.com
http://MirrorOfMotivation.com
http://BallOverseas.com
http://www.HoopHandbook.com/Free

2) Work On Your Game University

Work with Dre directly in his ONLY coaching program and meet with other members who are on your same journey.

Learn   More:
http://WorkOnYourGameUniversity.com

3) Work On Your Game LIVE

The LIVE events where you get all the BEST Work On Your Game material, all your questions answered and network with the like-minded people you want to associate with.

http://WorkOnYourGame.LIVE

4) Consigliere

An exclusive, invitation-only 1x1 program limited to 5 members at a time.

Support: Team@WorkOnMyGame.com | WorkOnYourGameUniversity.com | Text:1.305.384.6894

WORK ON YOUR GAME
UNIVERSITY

About The Author: Dre Baldwin

In just 5 years, Dre Baldwin went from the end of his high school team's bench, to the first contract of a 9-year professional basketball career.

While playing professional basketball, Dre pioneered new genres of personal branding and entrepreneurship via an ever-growing content publishing empire.

Dre started blogging in 2005 and began publishing videos to YouTube in 2006. He has published over 12,000 videos to 142,000+ subscribers, his content being viewed over 103 million times to date.

Dre's daily Work On Your Game Podcast MasterClass has over 2,800 episodes and more than 7.3 million downloads.

Dre has given 4 TEDxTalks on Discipline, Confidence, Mental Toughness & Personal Initiative and has authored 35 books. He has appeared in national campaigns with Nike, Finish Line, Wendy's, Gatorade, Buick, Wilson Sports, STASH Investments and DIME magazine.

A Philadelphia native, Dre lives in Miami.

Support: Team@WorkOnMyGame.com | WorkOnYourGameUniversity.com | Text:1.305.384.6894

Get The #MondayMotivation Text Every Week FREE!

Dre sends out a FREE text message every Monday that's guaranteed to have you focused, sharp and on-point to start your week.

Text now to join the community: **305.384.6894**. Normal texting rates apply.

Support: Team@WorkOnMyGame.com | WorkOnYourGameUniversity.com | Text:1.305.384.6894

Made in the USA
Columbia, SC
01 April 2024